To ... in the Lord, Be Blessed,
2012

Do You Want

Help

Or

What?

DAVID A BROGDON

TRUTH BOOK PUBLISHERS

First Printing – 2008
Second Revised Printing 2011
© David A. Brogdon 2004

COPYRIGHT NOTICE:

Address all Communication to:
David A. Brogdon
E-mail: DABrogdon@aol.com

All Scripture Quotes are from the
King James Version.

"Study to shew thyself approved unto God, a workman that needeth not to be ashamed, rightly dividing the word of truth."
—2 Timothy 2:15

ISBN 978-1-937089-07-8

Truth Book Publishers
824 Bills Rd
Franklin, IL 62638
877-649-9092
www.truthbookpublishers.com

A Very Special Thanks

To James and JaNell Lyle who have unselfishly given much to see this and other books come to fruition. As with Christ Jesus it is a debt that can never be paid. Also to Lyle Rogers for getting us started on the road to becoming an overcomer and "SPEAKING TO IT."

Do You Want Help
Or What!

ACKNOWLEDGEMENTS

To the Lord Jesus, for entering my life at an early age and revealing himself to me as Savior, Lord, and King. For His undying love for me, I am eternally grateful.

Many thanks are to be given to James and JaNell Lyle for their prompting of the writing of this book.

For my Mother, Donna Brogdon, and her dedication to review the tapes and transfer pages to written form was a great labor of love and without her help this would not be possible. May the Lord Jesus Christ bless their work and hands and give them the desires of their heart.

To my beautiful wife, Linda, for persevering the times the Lord had me out and about ministering and teaching. It is a blessing to have a soul mate so dedicated to the work of the Lord. I have truly found a virtuous woman as written in Proverbs 31:10, *"whose value is far above any jewels of this earth."* I will always love and cherish every moment together, thank you for being you!

To my two lovely daughters, Sheri and Heather, who have undergone the brunt of my learning experiences with Jesus? I love you both very much. You have made a father proud.

To my son-in-law, Matthew, for enduring the hours editing the context of this book and for his undying love for Jesus am grateful.

Do You Want

Help

Or

What?

DAVID A BROGDON

INTRODUCTION

When I was a lad, about 10, I read John 14:12-14 and saw something that later in my life changed the way I prayed. The Lord spoke to me and said; *"that, whatsoever ye shall ask of the Father in my name, he may give it you."* I began to see the importance of the Name of Jesus in my early walk. I thank Jesus for pulling me from the fire and setting my feet on the Rock.

We have been so misguided by erroneous teachings, by doctrines of man and devils. It is time the truth prevails. Light comes and darkness flees. Today there are many in the valley of decision according to Joel 3:14: *"Multitudes, multitudes in the valley of decision: for the day of the LORD is near in the valley of decision."*

Prayerfully, this small book will enlighten some and they shall begin the walk on the road of overcomers. I have found we are in a relationship and "IT'S EASY WITH JESUS."

David A. Brogdon

Chapter One

Dispelling Stinking Thinking!

There is a scripture that reveals in the last days many shall turn away from the truth. We see in 2 Timothy 4:4 *"And they shall turn away their ears from the truth, and shall be turned unto fables."*

Also written in 1Timothy 4:1

"Now the Spirit speaketh expressly, that in the latter times some shall depart from the faith, giving heed to seducing spirits, and doctrines of devils."

So what is Stinking Thinking? Listening to the many voices that takes us away from the Truth of the Word and cause us to walk without faith and loose our hope.

Do we not see this happening today? Many are going in another direction than the way of the Lord's. Many have begun to listen to another spirit other than the Holy Spirit. Many people are being led astray by men's doctrines. Many are in a place where they do not receive the truth.

Most believe they are taught the truth, but the evidence speaks for itself.

In this hour there are vessels the Lord is using to give truth and many do not receive because they are confused as to what is truth. What's needed is for people to begin to search the Scriptures for themselves. Finding the truth revealed in the Scriptures is our responsibility as believers. In Jesus Christ, the Word, is hidden the Truth. Develop the relationship and stay in Truth.

Timothy wanted to leave Ephesus because he was being bombarded with much garbage coming into the church. Many were excepting lies as the truth. Paul wrote Timothy and instructed him in 2 Timothy 2:15-16,

"Study to shew thyself approved unto God, a workman that needeth not to be ashamed, rightly dividing the word of truth. But shun profane and vain babblings: for they will increase unto more ungodliness."

There were those bringing in profane teachings and vain babblings causing the church to become weaker and weaker and non-effective. Today, in this hour of the church, we have the same thing happening. Because of this the church is anemic and weaker than ever before. Many shall fall in these last days because they chose to believe a lie rather than the truth. Many shall run after those who will tickle their ears and feed them a fable rather than the truth of God's word to strengthen them and cause them to grow into the likeness of Jesus. Even now many Shepherds have turned from pleasing God to pleasing man. This shall be there downfall.

2 Timothy 2:17 states;

"And their word will eat as doth a canker: of whom is Hymenaeus and Philetus."

False word is like a cancer it eats away at us. It is false and a lie, it will destroy faith. False teaching always destroys faith. Without faith it is impossible to please God (Hebrews 11:6). Many need to re-asses what is going on in their lives to see if they are getting the truth. It is needful this hour to walk with the Holy Spirit, walk in truth, teaching others to believe in the truth we have learned. We should be raising disciples to looking like the Lord Jesus Christ and not disciples looking like mortal men.

Satan and his devils have invaded most schools of theology in the world. There work is to water down the Gospel of the Kingdom making it non-effective, it has worked. Intellect has become the Gospel, a form of godliness but denying the power. Many deny healing, miracles, devils, and angels, always searching intellectually for the answer, as if they are to be found by reasoning. Our

15

society and church are full of the 'intellectual gospel'. Scripture informs us in 2 Timothy 3:5,

"Having a form of godliness, but denying the power thereof: from such turn away."

If they deny the things of the Lord, the supernatural, the baptism of the Holy Ghost…turn away from them.

The enemy of Father God, Satan (which should be our enemy), is doing quite a number on the saints. He, through his vessels of Balaam, are keeping the very best the Father has to offer, through His Son Jesus, from the saints.

Many have been taught from the pulpits in the world not to strive or contend for the Faith. They have been taught to settle for less than what Jesus died and rose again for—our inheritance. What is this Inheritance we have obtained from the resurrected Christ? We shall see, as it is unveiled for us in the next few chapters.

There are some of you who may be offended because of what you have read thus far. There may be those in ministry who may be upset and saying, "Why should I read this book?"

Do not get upset at me; get angry with Satan, the very one that some say does not exist, the one causing you to water down the Scriptures, the one causing the problems in your life and Church. If you think things are going all

16

right, they are not! Those of us in Ministry shall stand before a judgment seat in greater measure than those we teach. We shall give account for what we gave or did not give to those in our congregations.

WE SHALL GIVE AN ACCOUNT!

We need to be training, not controlling, the body of believers to flow in the Holy Ghost. The body needs to be trained to flow in the Spirit and His Gifts. They need to minister unto the Lord and the Body.

There are many people asking, "What are our gifts?" They have surveys to see if people have this gift or that gift. There are a lot of talents God has given us. But the Gifts are the prominent Gifts of the Holy Spirit (I Corinthians 12: 7-11). These Gifts should be evident in our lives. I believe this is for all of us this hour.

The young are eager and excited in this hour to step out and do something different. Quite honestly, it would be very difficult to go into some churches because it is so theologically and intellectually designed. There is no room for the Holy Spirit to move. It is so orchestrated and so timed. We place time restriction on the Holy Spirit. He has to move in this time frame only. Forty minutes of this day is what we are going to give Him. Maybe another forty minutes during the week or perhaps an hour.

Do not be offended by this. Just begin to open your ears and heart to the cry of the Spirit. The Scripture says, "Those who overcome have an ear to hear what the Spirit of God is saying to the Churches" (Revelation 2:7, 11, 17, 29; 3:6, 13, 22).

Overcome those barriers and obstacles that keep you from being what you could be in Jesus. Change your thinking. Change what schools of theology have given you. If it is not the truth, CHANGE IT!

Find the truth for yourself. Dispel the Stinking Thinking!

There is much for us to learn this hour. We, as the Church, need to do warfare. We, as the Church, need to understand that God will hold us accountable for our lack of participation. We have a foe, Satan. He is the foe of the Fathers' also. Through eons of time he has stolen many blessings from the Body of believers. It is time that we as the Body fights back, regain and restore what he has taken.

Jesus said in Matthew 11:12, *"And from the days of John the Baptist until now the kingdom of heaven suffereth violence, and the violent take it by force."* THIS IS THE KEY! Many do not want to fight and think we must love only. Yes, we need to love but we hate sin and must destroy the one who causes it. There is a great battle that shall come on the horizon. This battle will be between light and darkness… good and evil. Those of us who call upon the name of Jesus and are His followers, called Christians, need to stand up and get into this battle now!

We need to stand, be strong, and fight the good fight of FAITH.

The strongest force against Satan and his workers is the **Name of Jesus**. The Name of Jesus is a strong tower. Jesus is the Word and the Holy Ghost is the Spirit. It is the Word and the Spirit that will do the battle. As we take up the Word, the Name of Jesus, as we begin to use the Word of God (the Bible) against Satan, he must flee. How was Satan put away from Jesus when He was in wilderness, by speaking the words? *"It is written."*

We need to know and understand the written Word. We need to rid ourselves of thinking that brings in doubt and unbelief. Many congregations and prayer meetings pray mostly for their own selfish things. We do not see what is going on around us only what is in our world. We have no recognition of the battle in the heavenlies. We need to change our lives and change the way we think and change the way we pray.

Satan can never defeat Jesus because Jesus defeated him and took all his keys from him. Jesus, then, gave us the keys to use against Satan. The number one key is His name! It is the most important of all. THE NAME OF JESUS! For when we use the name of Jesus it brings to the Father's memory what Jesus did for us at the cross and how Jesus defeated the enemy and the works of darkness. It also reminds the Father that He gave all power and authority unto Jesus. And Jesus, in turn, gave it to us. When we say the name of Jesus, the Father knows that all power was turned over to His Son, (Matthew 28:18), *"And Jesus came and spake unto them, saying, 'All power is given unto me in heaven and in earth.'"*

And Jesus turned around and gave it to us as believers, (Acts 1:8),

"But ye shall receive power, after that the Holy Ghost is come upon you: and ye shall be witnesses unto me both in Jerusalem, and in all Judea, and in Samaria, and unto the uttermost part of the earth."

And He said in Luke 10:19 that we have power over the enemy and nothing shall hurt us. Why do we fear?

"Behold, I give unto you power to tread on serpents and scorpions, and over all the power of the enemy: and nothing shall by any means hurt you."

FEAR NOT!

What a glorious inheritance we have now in the Name of Jesus. Right now! At the time you are reading this book, you have an inheritance in Jesus. Hallelujah!!

Most people have been taught that this was for the disciples, the early Christians, but not for us today. How sad this is? It is sad because we have been robbed from a blessing. Have you ever wondered about your earthly inheritance from parents, grandparents or any loved ones? You have to wait till they die to receive. Then we go through lawyers and relatives and by the time it is done we feel so drained, tired, hurt and disappointed, even sometimes rejected.

It is the same today in the Church. So many have robbed us from our spiritual inheritance saying this is not for today. Some say you have to be so holy to receive these things. Others say you have to wait till you get to heaven.

If this were true then Jesus died in vain. Jesus rose again. He is not hanging on the cross! We see many pictures with Jesus hanging on the cross, and it is wonderful that He went to the cross, praise God that was His destiny. It was His earthly journey to take upon Himself all our sins, transgressions and iniquities. As we ask Jesus into our life, we can renounce these things in His Name. We can break free.

So Jesus is not on the cross today! We need to get a new picture of that in our mind. Thank God for the cross, Paul says, but Jesus did not stay there. He was brought down from the cross and put in the grave. He was three days in the grave but He arose again. This is the glorious story. This is where our inheritance begins. JESUS ROSE AGAIN! Because He rose again we have this glorious inheritance, right now! We do not have to wait. For those who do not know or have no experience with Jesus Christ this is the time. Paul states in 2 Corinthians 6:2;

"For he saith, I have heard thee in a time accepted, and in the day of salvation have I succoured thee: behold, now is the day of salvation."

Ask Jesus now to come into your heart and be Savior, Lord and King. Repent of your sins. So shall you be **'born again'** and **'saved'** from the destruction to come. Begin to use His name in a proper way, not in a derogatory way.

If you have done this, repent now. Ask for forgiveness. Call upon the Name of Jesus. Call upon the Name that is above all names, Jesus and believe on Him. Believe on Jesus Christ, the One who rose from the grave. Because of His resurrection power, we have resurrection power. He has given us our inheritance, NOW. There is never any disappointment in Jesus. He wants to heal us, not hurt us. To give us strength, not wear us out. To bless us, not curse us. This wonderful Name **Jesus**, the King, the Lord, and the Savior. What a glorious Name...**JESUS**!

We shall go through some battles, though this is not what we like to hear. We have been taught we will not go through them. This is an erroneous teaching. We shall go through but with **Jesus' name** we can win. We need to study about Jesus' provision for us as we do battle this hour against our enemy, Satan.

As we call upon the Name of Jesus, the Holy Spirit will guide us. He will lead us to the Truth. Pray this daily.

In the Book of John 16: 13; Jesus said, *"Howbeit when he, the Spirit of Truth, is come, He will guide you into all truth: for he shall not speak of Himself; but whatsoever he shall hear, that shall He speak: and He will show you things to come."*

What a blessing. The Holy Spirit begins to show us things to come. Thank God for the Holy Spirit, the Third Person of the Godhead, that reveals and shows us things. He brings us to the **truth**.

You find in Matthew 16: 13-16, *"When Jesus came into the coasts of Caesarea Philippi, he asked his disciples, saying, Whom do men say that I the Son of man am? And they said, Some say that thou art John the Baptist: some, Elias; and others, Jeremias, or one of the prophets. He saith unto them, But whom say ye that I am? And*

Simon Peter answered and said, Thou art the Christ, the Son of the living God."

The Spirit of Truth led Peter into truth. We need **Truth** in this hour more than ever before. Let us rely on the Holy Spirit to lead us as Peter did.

Look in John 14: 16-18,

"And I will pray the Father, and he shall give you another Comforter, that he may abide with you for ever; Even the Spirit of truth; whom the world cannot receive."

The world cannot receive the Spirit of Truth because they do not believe on Jesus. For those of you reading this book, believe on Jesus [so shall you be saved] and receive the Spirit of Truth. Go further on than others in the church. Even for those who are Spirit baptized there is more. There is so much more. MOVE ON!

The Holy Spirit is prompting many to go on to a victorious life in Jesus. We can move forward in Christ Jesus. Yes, we will fight battles and might loose a little ground here and there but the total outcome is we shall win. We shall win. We shall overcome.

So pray for the baptism in the Holy Spirit. Jesus is the mighty baptizer in the Holy Spirit. Call upon His Name and ask to be filled with the Holy Spirit with evidence in tongues as the early Church.

People that are saved have the Holy Spirit. But they have not received the Baptism of the Holy Spirit. They have not received the full infilling of the Holy Spirit the evidence is in tongues. The early men of faith believed in the Baptism of the Holy Ghost with tongues as the evidence. We need to go forth in the power and might of the Holy Spirit in our lives. ***"I will not leave you comfortless: I will come to you."***

Jesus is returning again and we need to grow today in Him. Grow in the Spirit of the Lord. We need to check what comes from the pulpit. Check to see if there is error in teaching. You ministers who are teaching the Word shall be held accountable in what you give. To stand before the judgment seat humbles me to think, the very things I give you better be the **truth**.

In John 8:31,

"Then said Jesus to those Jews which believed on him, If ye continue in my word, then are ye my disciples indeed; and you shall know the Truth and the Truth shall set you free."

Truth is something we desperately need in this hour. Earlier we saw that the devil comes with doctrines that are not of the Lord. Man likes his own doctrines also. What does man's doctrines do, brings about spiritual death?

The writer of Hebrews 6: 1-3 states: *"Therefore leaving the principles of the doctrine of Christ, let us go on unto perfection;* (maturity). Many in the body of Christ are mature in age but not mature in the Spirit. This is the hour that we need to be growing and becoming mature spiritually, *"...not laying again the foundation of repentance from dead works, and of faith toward God, Of the doctrine of baptisms, and of laying on of hands, and of resurrection of the dead, and of eternal judgment. And this will we do, if God permit."* This is the principle of the doctrines of Christ, laying that firm foundation. Being built upon the Rock and foundation, which is Jesus Christ.

We need to repent from our dead works. If it is a religious service we are going through than it is dead works. We need to repent and go on. We need to have faith towards God and faith in God. Believe that His Word is true.

We need to believe in the doctrine of baptisms. There is baptism of water and baptism of the Holy Spirit. We need these baptisms in our lives. There are some that will never get these. But we need these in our lives as overcomers.

Concerning the resurrection of the dead, when Lazarus was in the grave and Mary said to Jesus, *"Lord, I know he* [Lazarus] *shall rise up in the resurrection of the dead...."* She knew as many people know there is going to be a resurrection and we need this hope. Those who have their hope in Him must strive to live a life that would be pleasing unto Him.

We shall see the resurrection and eternal judgment. A lot of people do not like to hear about judgment. People say we should not judge. But we need to judge! Paul says if we are to judge angels (I Corinthians 6:3) how much more should we judge what is going on in the body. We need to judge righteous judgment. Judge by the Spirit; know by the Spirit, being led by the Spirit. God desires for us to flow with the Spirit.

Paul, in Ephesians 4:11 saw the body of believers would not come to the full measure of Christ, into unity of faith, unless something happened.

"And he gave some, apostles; and some, prophets; and some, evangelists; and some, pastors and teachers; for the perfecting (maturing) of the saints for the work of the ministry."

We must work in our ministries to build up the body of Christ coming into unity of faith and knowledge of the Son of God unto maturity, unto the stature and measure of the fullness of Christ. We need ministries of power and authority, today! God is restoring in this hour. There are true apostles, prophets, evangelists, teachers, and shepherds being raised up of God who have a heart to bring His people into the knowledge of the **truth**.

Paul says we can come into this full measure of the fullness of Christ. We have the ability if we allow the servants God is raising up to bring us to the fullness. There were female prophetesses in the Old Testament. There can be female prophetess today and not with a Jezebel spirit. There is so much fear about Jezebel today. We, like Elisha, need to rise up and prophesy over the Jezebel spirits this hour and pull down their power in the churches, this nation, and in nations around about in Jesus' Name.

Paul goes on in Ephesians 4:14,

"That we henceforth be no more children tossed to and fro and carried about every wind of doctrine by the craftiness of men where by they lie in wait to deceive us."

The very first thing Jesus said in Matthew 24:4, when the disciples asked Jesus to give them an understanding in what is going to happen in the last days. The very first thing that Jesus said was, *"Take heed that no man deceive you."*

This is the word for the last days. It is the sign of the coming and the end of this world deception is on the rise. People led by demons have deceived us into believing the lie.

Paul goes on in Ephesians 4:15,

"But speaking the truth in love, may grow up into him in all things, which is the head, even Christ: from whom the whole body fitly joined together and compacted by that which every joint supplies according to the effectual work and the measure of every part maketh increase to the body and to the edifying of itself in love."

The body is coming together out of darkness. The blinders are being spiritually removed off our eyes so we can see and understand the truth. The Spirit of God is opening our ears this hour to hear the TRUTH.

Thank Jesus for the Truth.

Matthew 24:13 states: *"But he that shall endure unto the end, the same shall be saved."* We need to endure or stay put no matter what comes our direction stand in the name of Jesus. Paul gave us an understanding of this in Ephesians 6:13:

"Wherefore take unto you the whole armour of God, that ye may be able to withstand in the evil day, and having done all, to stand. Stand therefore, having your loins girt about with truth, and having on the breastplate of righteousness."

We should stand with the Truth around us. When you have done ALL, stand. Stand for truth and don't back down. We are not to back up from the enemy but speak the truth and he must flee.

Paul, in his discourse to the church of Philippi, stated in Philippians 4:13: *"I can do all things through Christ which strengtheneth me."*

If we are in Christ Jesus nothing shall be impossible to us, because nothing is impossible to God. As Gabriel was speaking to Mary and stated to her, *"For with God nothing shall be impossible"* (Luke 1:37).

Jesus, in talking with his disciples, declared it was their unbelief that hindered them. In Matthew 17: 20: *"And Jesus said unto them, 'Because of your unbelief: for verily I say unto you, If you have faith as a grain of mustard seed, ye shall say unto this mountain, Remove hence to yonder place; and it shall remove; and nothing shall be impossible unto you."*

We can reach the impossible with Jesus having only a mustard seed of faith!

Remove the **Stinking Thinking** and move forward in mountain moving faith!

Let us pray together and ask the Father to forgive us of any wrong thinking we may have had.

PRAYER

Father, in the name of Jesus your Son and our Lord and Savior, please forgive me for being influenced by wrong teaching or any doctrine of man or the devil. I recognize there may be some areas in my life that have been corrupted by an alien source, causing me to think differently than your Word. I desire to move up in the Spirit to the level you have always wanted me to attain. Change my thinking to line up with your Word. This day I choose to believe your Word and to try the spirits that would influence me to go another direction away from your very best for me. In the name of Jesus, remove from me any stinking thinking that causes doubt and disbelief of your Word. It is written I am the righteousness of God in Christ Jesus and all things are possible to him who believes. From this moment on I choose to believe.

Amen.

Chapter Two

Let's Deal with Our Inheritance!

God is restoring TRUTH in these last days. Restoring Truth that will equip the Body for the return of our Lord and Savior Jesus Christ.

How many of us have inherited something we did not want?

I want to talk about an inheritance I did not want and that is the Iniquities of my forefathers.

Turn to Ezra 9. Ezra, the priest, was bringing Judah out of captivity. They were restoring the walls (foundation Truth).They were restoring the temple (Holiness). Ezra, the priest, was reading the Word and saw many things and Ezra, the priest, wept because of Israel's sins, transgressions, and iniquities.

Ezra 9:5-8:

And at the evening sacrifice I arose up from my heaviness; and having rent my garment and my mantle, I fell upon my knees, and spread out my hands unto the LORD my God, And said, O my God, I am ashamed and blush to lift up my face to thee, my God: for our iniquities are increased over our head, and our trespass is grown up unto the heavens. Since the days of our fathers have we been in a great trespass unto this day; and for our iniquities have we, our kings, and our priests, been delivered into the hand of the kings of the lands, to the sword, to captivity, and to a spoil, and to confusion of face, as it is this day. And now for a little space grace hath been shewed from the LORD our God, to leave us a remnant to escape, and to give us a nail in his holy place, that our God may lighten our eyes, and give us a little reviving in our bondage.

"I am ashamed and blushed because of the iniquities of my forefathers." Can you imagine this man of God lying before God, confessing the sins, iniquities and the transgressions of the people? We need men of God to rise up today to confess the sins, iniquities and transgressions of the people.

Iniquity, I believe, is the root of all generational curses. In Exodus 20, the Ten Commandments were given and we find where iniquities were passed down.

Exodus 20:1-6

And God spake all these words, saying, I am the LORD thy God, which have brought thee out of the land of Egypt, out of the house of bondage. Thou shalt have no other gods before me. Thou shalt not make unto thee any graven image, or any likeness of any thing that is *in heaven above, or that is in the earth beneath, or that is in the water under the earth: Thou shalt not bow down thyself to them, nor serve them: for I the LORD thy God am a jealous God, visiting the iniquity of the fathers upon the children unto the third and fourth generation of them that hate me; And shewing mercy unto thousands of them that <u>love</u> me, and keep my commandments.*

God wants to show mercy to us today. What is MERCY?

God is **M**aking **E**verything **R**ight **C**oncerning **Y**ou.

God is restoring His people and He has a remnant who will listen. Those who have ears to hear what the Spirit is saying, are doers of the Word, these are the remnant. They are overcomers. Do you want in that group?

We talk a lot about our sins. We repent and cry out to God over our sins. But, our transgressions are not spoken of much. Iniquity is hardly spoken about at all.

Iniquity is the Greek word, *Avone*, which means "perverseness, to be bent or crooked, to be run out of course"; it signifies not that which is wrong but the tendency to do wrong. This inclination lies in our disposition and nature not merely in the act of the transgression of the law. It is nothing less than the spirit and nature of the devil working in the children of disobedience.

God, in His mercy, wants and is bringing His remnant out of this nature.

Webster's Dictionary states that iniquity is "gross injustice." The word "injustice" means "a violation of a right or the rights of another, an act that inflicts undeserved hurt."

If iniquity is passed down to us it inflicts undeserved hurt from sin. It inflicts something in our lives. Ezra enlightened us to see we are turned over to the Kings of the land because of iniquities. Kings of the land (Satan) has a legal right to inflict things upon us because of our inherited iniquities.

Many of us have taken care of "sin." Sin is an offense against a religious or moral law, to commit an offense or a fault; an act of stumbling or a breach of moral or social code or misdemeanor.

Sin is you did not know and you are sorry. Forgive me.

What is a transgression? It is "to go beyond the limits set or prescribed by or to violate a command or a law."

What is a transgression today? "I know it is wrong but I am going to do it anyway."

Iniquity, that "gross injustice" which means there is an inward drive that is compelling me to sin and to transgress the Word of God.

Isaiah 53:4-5:

"Surely he hath borne our grief's, and carried our sorrows: yet we did esteem him stricken, smitten of God, and afflicted.   But he was wounded for our <u>transgressions</u>, he was bruised for our <u>iniquities</u>: the chastisement of our peace was upon him; and with his stripes we are healed."

People in the Body of Christ do not know the distinctions between the terminologies of sins, transgressions and iniquities. Because of this, everything is lumped under sin. "I have sinned against God!"

How many times did Jesus bleed for us? Seven times! Where did He bleed? First, in the Garden He sweat blood. He was asking God to forgive us for our weakness. It came off His head so He bled for our mental weakness. We are weak in our minds. He bled for us in the Garden so that our wills could be changed by the power of His blood. Then Jesus was taken into captivity and the soldiers made Him a crown and placed it on His head and smote Him, the thorns were driven into His head. He bled. By His blood He wants to deliver our mind, will and emotions and desires. He wants to set us free.

As He was crucified on the cross they put nails into His hands. He bled from His hands for the work we do with our hands. Do we do all things as unto the Lord? I doubt not. All of our work should be done as unto the Lord.

He bled from His feet. Our feet take us places. It is our walk in life. He wants our walk in life to be clean. He wants it to be pure.

He bled from His side. A sword was thrust into His side. It speaks of our transgressions. He wants to heal and deliver us from the curse of transgressions.

He bled from His back where He was beaten. "With His stripes we are healed."

When Jesus was on the cross, the blood and the water from His side fell to the earth. God was redeeming the earth (humans through the Blood of the Lamb). We are a lump of clay (earth) and God is the potter. He is bringing us out of idolatry out of the world system. We are in the world but not to be like the world.

I believe the primary cause of lukewarmness in the body of Christ is we have not dealt with internal torments caused by iniquities.

There were outward signs of blood while He was on the cross. But He was also bruised for our iniquities. A bruise is a blood vessel that has been broken that is under the skin. One thing about a bruise is it can be covered. That's the way with us, transgressions that lead to iniquities get covered over and we do not deal with them. If there is something that compels you to sin all the time, there is an iniquity that is in your bloodline and needs to be broken.

Exodus 34:6-7:

"And the LORD passed by before him, and proclaimed, The LORD, The LORD God, merciful and gracious, longsuffering, and abundant in goodness and truth, Keeping mercy for thousands, forgiving iniquity and transgression and sin, and that will by no means clear the guilty; visiting the iniquity of the fathers upon the children, and upon the children's children, unto the third and to the fourth generation."

The iniquities are being visited upon us now.

Leviticus 16:20-22:

"And when he hath made an end of reconciling the holy place, and the tabernacle of the congregation, and the altar, he shall bring the live goat: And Aaron shall lay both his hands upon the head of the live goat, and confess over him all the iniquities of the children of Israel, and all their transgressions in all their sins, putting them upon the head of the goat, and shall send him away by the hand of a fit man into the wilderness: And the goat shall bear upon him all their

iniquities unto a land not inhabited: and he shall let go the goat in the wilderness."

Here is the High Priest confessing all the sins, transgressions and iniquities on this goat. This was a scapegoat. Jesus today is our scapegoat.

Is salvation for everyone? Yes! Is everyone saved? No! Why, because they never ask?

Is healing for everyone? Yes! Is everyone healed? No! Why, because we do not ask. Some believe that God put sickness upon them. He may have allowed it (like Job) but it was not His intent for it to remain forever.

Is everyone delivered? No!

Even though Jesus became a curse for us, we need to appropriate His Word over our circumstances. If we do not appropriate, we will never receive our total freedom. It would have been nice at our conversion to have been saved, healed, delivered and made a holy vessel right then and never to sin again. Wouldn't that have been great? But it did not happen that way. The Lord in His mercy took us anyway, warts and all. He can still use an unclean vessel as long as we strive to be made clean.

Iniquities are shackles that hold us down so we are never free. There is a verse in Revelation 12:11 that states in part, *"they overcame him by the blood, by the word of our testimony and loving not our lives as unto death."*

People love their lives too much to let go of it. We need to let go of our life. It is not ours any longer if we have been bought with the high price of Christ Jesus' blood.

Job went through many things yet Job never sinned against God.

Job 13:23-26:

"How many are mine <u>iniquities</u> and sins? make me to know my <u>transgression</u> and my <u>sin</u>. Wherefore hidest thou thy face, and holdest me for thine enemy? Wilt thou break a leaf driven to and fro? and wilt thou pursue the dry stubble? For thou writest bitter things against me, and makest me to possess the iniquities of my youth."

How many iniquities have we received from our youth and our forefathers?

Psalm 32:1-5:

"Blessed is he whose transgression is forgiven, whose sin is covered. Blessed is the man unto whom the LORD imputeth not iniquity, and in whose spirit there is no guile. When I kept silence, my bones waxed old through my roaring all the day long. For day and night thy hand was heavy upon me: my moisture is turned into the drought of summer. Selah. I acknowledged my <u>sin</u> unto thee, and mine iniquity have I not hid. I said, I will confess my <u>transgressions</u> unto the LORD; and thou forgavest the <u>iniquity</u> of my sin. Selah" (Stop and think on this.*)*

41

David was saying, "I acknowledge that I have sinned. I acknowledge that I have willfully sinned which became an iniquity. I knew it was wrong but I did it anyway. I transgressed against You. I willfully did it."

Isaiah 59:1-4:

"Behold, the LORD's hand is not shortened, that it cannot save; neither his ear heavy, that it cannot hear: But your iniquities have separated between you and your God, and your sins have hid his face from you, that he will not hear. For your hands are defiled with blood, and your fingers with iniquity; your lips have spoken lies, your tongue hath muttered perverseness. None calleth for justice, nor any pleadeth for truth: they trust in vanity, and speak lies; they conceive mischief, and bring forth iniquity."

Thank God that His hand is not shortened that it cannot save us. The word "save" means deliver. Can He deliver us today from the iniquities of our forefathers? Have there been some things in your life that you cannot get from underneath? You have sinned and willfully did it. There was something that compelled you to do those things. When you did it, you just felt miserable. Then you did it again and again. You cried unto the Lord but it still kept happening. I believe we need to confess the iniquities of our forefathers. Sin lies at the door but God has a Truth He wants to show us how to go through the door. He wants to bring us through to the other side.

What happened at the first Passover? Look in Exodus 12. They had to put blood on the door. It says they had to kill a lamb in Verse 7: *"And they shall take of the blood, and strike it on the two side posts and on the upper door post of the houses, wherein they shall eat it."*

- The Blood is for our sin. (Side of doorpost) [Flesh]
- The Blood is for our transgression. (Side of doorpost) [Soul]
- The Blood is for our iniquity. (Upper lintel) [Spirit]

These Three areas we need to deal with; Sin, Transgression and Iniquity. The blood covered all of this but we need to appropriate the blood. Just like the Israelites had to appropriate the blood. They did it during the Passover. We must appropriate the blood for our life. We must apply the blood over areas of our life, because if we leave any door open, then iniquity will be able to come back. We have to appropriate the blood and close the door once and for all on our sins, transgressions, and iniquities.

Proverbs 16:6:

"By mercy and truth iniquity is purged: and by the fear of the LORD men depart from evil."

We need truth and mercy of God to purge us from iniquity. Truth knows how to apply the blood to the areas of our life where there is sin, transgressions and iniquities. Some say, "I really like this sin." Some people do like their sin. They say, "It's not a bad sin." "I didn't tell a bad lie." A lie is a lie. Beguilement is beguilement!

Jesus is our High Priest who removes our iniquities and is the Word personified.

Hebrews 4:12-13:

"For the <u>word</u> of God is quick, and powerful, and sharper than any two-edged sword, piercing even to the dividing asunder of soul and spirit, and of the joints and marrow, and is a discerner of the thoughts and intents of the heart. Neither is there any creature that is not manifest in his sight: but all things are naked and opened unto the eyes of him with whom we have to do."

All things are opened to Jesus. He knows your sins, your transgressions, and your iniquities.

Do you know what went on four generations ago in your bloodline? No one does! We have no idea. I was fortunate to sit with my grandparents one time and they told me of a few generations back from them. So I had the opportunity to go back three generations and found out some of the transgressions, sins, and iniquities of my forefathers and brought them under the blood of Jesus

Christ once and for all to do away with them. My wife and I prayed with our children, out loud so Satan knew that we knew. My daughters have since said that they really appreciate that we did this with them because it saved them from many hurts.

"Seeing then that we have a great high priest, that is passed into the heavens, Jesus the Son of God, let us hold fast our profession. For we have not an high priest which cannot be touched with the feeling of our infirmities; but was in all points tempted like as we are, yet without sin."

Jesus was the Unleavened Bread.

We do not know which side of the bloodline iniquities comes from but they come anyway. It is as though someone comes to beat us up in certain areas of our life and we do not know how to deal with it. We need to be cleansed from it. We need to confess it before the Lord, our God.

Psalm 103:1-6:

"Bless the LORD, O my soul: and all that is within me, bless his holy name. Bless the LORD, O my soul, and forget not all his benefits: Who forgiveth all thine iniquities; who healeth all thy diseases; Who redeemeth thy life from destruction; who crowneth thee with loving kindness and tender mercies; Who satisfieth thy mouth with good things; so that thy youth is renewed like the eagle's. The

LORD executeth righteousness and judgment for all that are oppressed."

God wants to heal us. I believe iniquities cause diseases in our bodies, which we need healing for. I believe sin causes diseases in our bodies. We need to get to the root of our problems. When we go to the doctor, the doctor asks many questions. He wants to get to the root of your problem. Did anyone in your family have heart disease? Did anyone in your family have any blood disease? So it is with us as Christians. We need to go to the root of these things, break the curse of it so we can be healed once and for all.

There are certain sins and transgressions that require the death penalty in the Word of God. But God in His mercy has spared us. Thank God for His mercy. If there were no mercy then there would be no human race.

Lamentations 5:1-8:

"Remember, O LORD, what is come upon us: consider, and behold our reproach. Our inheritance is turned to strangers, our houses [our temples—bodies] *to aliens* [demons]."

If you have iniquities in your life than you have aliens (demons) within and you need to be set free. The word alien is used in alienate. It wants to separate you from the anointing, separate you from holiness and keep you in darkness and they want to keep you perverse and in sin.

"We are orphans and fatherless, our mothers are as widows. We have drunken our water for money; our wood is sold unto us. Our necks are under persecution: we labour, and have no rest. We have given the hand to the Egyptians, and to the Assyrians, to be satisfied with bread. Our fathers have sinned, and are not; and we have borne their iniquities. Servants (aliens) have ruled over us: there is none that doth deliver us out of their hand."

Those of you who have illnesses, iniquity is behind that. If you are having problems in your finances and you are doing everything that is prescribed in the Word of God and you are still having problems in your finances there is iniquity behind that. That curse needs to be broken.

Psalm 106:1-6:

"Praise ye the LORD. O give thanks unto the LORD; for he is good: for his mercy endureth for ever. Who can utter the mighty acts of the LORD? Who can shew forth all his praise? Blessed are they that keep judgment, and he that doeth righteousness at all times. Remember me, O LORD, with the favour that thou bearest unto thy people: O visit me with thy salvation; That I may see the good of thy chosen, that I may rejoice in the gladness of thy nation, that I may glory with thine inheritance. We have sinned with our fathers, we have committed iniquity, we have done wickedly."

Here we find David remembering what his forefathers had done. He is saying to the Lord, "Remember the righteous things that I have done, for Your mercy is not slack today. Your mercy is forever and ever."

Jesus, thank You for Your mercy.

We have all at one time or another sinned. The scripture says, "All have sinned and come short of the glory of God."

I have been in the glory twice. You cannot stand in the glory because the glory consumes you. Anything that is not of God will be brought forth. He will show you the areas of iniquity and sin in your life.

I recall being in a meeting and the fire of God came into the meeting. We could not stand to minister because of the fire of God. People were saying all around, "It's burning, it's burning." God was burning the things out of us. Then the Word of the Lord came. It was awesome what the Lord had to say to us. He said He would continue to cleanse us and continue to make us holy vessels. We wept because of the Word of the Lord. Very few weep over the Word today.

When Ezra and Nehemiah were restoring the temple and Israel was restoring the wall, there was a reading of the Word. When the Word was read all stood for one-fourth part of the day. The reading of the Word moved them all.

Psalm 51:1-12:

"Have mercy upon me, O God, according to thy loving kindness: according unto the multitude of thy tender mercies blot out my transgressions. Wash me thoroughly from mine iniquity, and cleanse me from my <u>sin</u>. For I acknowledge my transgressions: and my <u>sin</u> is ever before me. Against thee, thee only, have I sinned, and done this evil in thy sight: that thou mightest be justified when thou speakest, and be clear when thou judgest. Behold, I was shapen in <u>iniquity</u>; and in sin did my mother conceive me. Behold, thou desirest truth in the inward parts: and in the hidden part thou shalt make me to know wisdom. Purge me with hyssop, and I shall be clean: wash me, and I shall be whiter than snow. Make me to hear joy and gladness; that the bones which thou hast broken may rejoice. Hide thy face from my sins, and blot out all mine iniquities. Create in me a clean heart, O God; and renew a right spirit within me."

This is where the church should be headed having a new spirit within us, should be operating via the Holy Spirit.

Cast me not away from thy presence; and take not thy holy spirit from me. This should be our cry today. We need the Holy Spirit to help us.

Restore unto me the joy of thy salvation; and uphold me with thy free spirit. We need to be cleansed.

God is no respecter of persons. If He cleanses one, He will cleanse all.

Iniquity is like a pinball game where our fathers have transgressed against God. Satan controls the levers and drops the little balls in the holes to keep iniquity going for another three or four generations. He plays with us. When things begin to happen; poverty, sickness, or whatever, we know the devil has a contract against us to steal, kill and destroy us.

What did Jesus do? He came to give us life and that more abundantly. Today is the day of restoration!!

Let us go to Matthew 24. Jesus was telling the disciples about the end times. Today, people want to know about the end times.

Matthew 24:4

"And Jesus answered and said unto them, Take heed that no man deceive you."

Deception is rampant in the Body of Christ because people do not have ears to hear what the Spirit is saying.

Matthew 24:11-12:

"And many false prophets shall rise, and shall deceive many. And because iniquity shall abound, the love of many shall wax cold."

Has your love grown cold toward your Lord and Savior, Jesus? Is iniquity in your life today? Do you need deliverance? Iniquity will cause you to leave the presence of God. It will cause the presence of God to go from you. Iniquity is abounding in the Body of Christ. That is why so many are lukewarm today. Iniquity will grow in your life till you become lukewarm.

II Thessalonians 2:2-4:

"That ye be not soon shaken in mind, or be troubled, neither by spirit, nor by word, nor by letter as from us, as that the day of Christ is at hand. Let no man deceive you by any means: for that day shall not come, except there come a falling away first, and that man of sin be revealed, the son of perdition; Who opposeth and exalteth himself above all that is called God, or that is worshipped; so that he as God sitteth in the temple [naos—we are the temple] *of God, shewing himself that he is God."*

Let me show you what the temple really is in these verses.

1 Corinthians 3:16-17

"Know ye not that ye are the temple [naos] *of God, and that the Spirit of God dwelleth in you? If any man defile the temple* [naos] *of God, him shall God destroy; for the temple* [naos] *of God is holy, which temple* [naos] *ye are."*

Naos is the Greek word for temple.

2 Thessalonians 2:4 is not referring to a building but to our body as the temple. Who is going to sit in this temple

(us) and exalt himself—the man of sin within? The iniquitous one is sitting there. He knows its sin but he is going to do it any way. He is going to exalt himself and say that he is God.

This is the end of the matter. Iniquity is going to grow and grow until finally you are going to set yourself up and oppose all things that are of God. Perhaps there are some of you who have already started in this direction. You oppose some of the true teachings of God. Some say we do not need deliverance today.

Some say we do not need healing today: "I am suffering these things for Christ's sake!" Some say that God has put sickness on them so that they might suffer for Him. **This is false.**

The only one suffering is the person who is ill. Jesus is not glorified in your suffering but in your healing so you might manifest your healing and tell others what He has done for you.

God knows our lineage. He knows those in our lineage who have been charged with iniquities. Thank God for Jesus' blood because His blood will obliterate those iniquities. He wants to blot out the sin of iniquity in our lives. If there is a stain in some clothing what do you do? You have to bleach it or put stain remover on it. This is what Jesus wants to do today. He wants to blot it out and remove the stain, the iniquities. As long as an iniquity remains there is a remembrance of it.

Jeremiah 31:33-34:

"But this shall be the covenant that I will make with the house of Israel; After those days, saith the LORD, I will put my law in their inward parts, and write it in their hearts; and will be their God, and they shall be my people. And they shall teach no more every man his neighbour, and every man his brother, saying, Know the LORD: for they shall all know me, from the least of them unto the greatest of them, saith the LORD: for I will forgive their iniquity, and I will remember their sin no more."

Again in Hebrews it says the same thing; Hebrews 8:10 and 10:16, 17"

"This is the covenant that I will make with them after those days, saith the Lord, I will put my laws into their hearts, and in their minds will I write them; And their sins and iniquities will I remember no more."

Have you ever said, "I have always been this way"? "I have always had this problem." "Every year at this time I get sinus problems." Sinus problems are rooted in idolatry. Your ancestors were in idolatry or perhaps you are and do not know it.

God said that when He brought the Israelites out of Egypt that He would not put any of the diseases of Egypt upon them…if they obeyed Him. This was the key. Obedience is better than sacrifice.

Deuteronomy 28:1-14 are the blessings and 28: 15-68 are the curses. There are more curses than blessings.

Deuteronomy 28:45-48

"Moreover all these curses shall come upon thee, and shall pursue thee, and overtake thee, till thou be destroyed; because thou hearkenedst not unto the voice of the LORD thy God, to keep his commandments and his statutes which he commanded thee: And they shall be upon thee for a sign and for a wonder, and upon thy seed for ever. Because thou servedst not the LORD thy God with joyfulness, and with gladness of heart, for the abundance of all things; Therefore shalt thou serve thine enemies which the LORD shall send against thee, in hunger, and in thirst, and in nakedness, and in want of all things: and he shall put a yoke of iron upon thy neck, until he have destroyed thee."

Deuteronomy 28:58-61

"If thou wilt not observe to do all the words of this law that are written in this book, that thou mayest fear this glorious and fearful name, THE LORD THY GOD."

We do not fear the Lord today. Certain countries fear the Lord. Down in South America they call Him Mr. Jesus.

"Then the LORD will make thy plagues wonderful, and the plagues of thy seed, even great plagues, and of long continuance, and sore sicknesses, and of long continuance. Moreover he will bring upon thee all the diseases of Egypt, which thou wast afraid of; and they shall cleave unto thee. Also every sickness, and every plague, which is not written in the book of this law, them will the LORD bring upon thee, until thou be destroyed."

Why, because they did not obey the commandments and the statutes? What are the commandments today? Love the Lord thy God with all thy heart and love thy neighbor as thyself. If you do not love yourself, you will not love your neighbor.

We find that there will be sickness placed upon us because we did not obey God. We see today there are many with sicknesses upon them because of the iniquities of the forefathers.

God made a special covenant with His people. He pulled them out of darkness and delivered them. He remembered their sins and iniquities no more because they confessed them. Today He will do the same through Jesus.

Sometimes we do not know what happened three and four generations ago. So we need to confess everything. Iniquity has to be purged from us.

Proverbs 16:6

"By mercy and truth iniquity is purged: and by the fear of the LORD men depart from evil."

Mercy and Truth deliver us! Fear of the Lord keeps us delivered.

God is today purging us to thoroughly cleanse us. That is why we need the blood of Christ poured over our conscience and our mind, so our thinking is changed. We must serve the Living God in fear.

People say they do not go to church because there is hypocrisy there. They see the churchgoers say one thing on Sunday and live another way during the week. So, I say to them, come on in anyway because the Lord might use you to change us.

Leviticus 26:39-42

"And they that are left of you shall pine away in their iniquity in your enemies' lands; and also in the iniquities of their fathers shall they pine away with them. If they shall confess their iniquity, and the iniquity of their fathers, with their trespass which they trespassed against me, and that also they have walked contrary unto me; And that I also have walked contrary unto them, and have brought them into the land of their enemies; if then their uncircumcised hearts be humbled, and they then accept of the punishment of their iniquity: Then will I remember my covenant with Jacob, and also my covenant with Isaac, and also my

covenant with Abraham will I remember; and I will remember the land."

There are seven things we need to look into.

1. Confess our own iniquities.

2. Confess the iniquities of our fathers and the trespass that they committed against God.

3. We need to admit that our fathers and forefathers walked contrary to God.

4. We need to admit that God is righteous and walks contrary to us because of our forefather's iniquities and those we brought upon ourselves.

5. We need to acknowledge that God has brought us into captivity into the land of our enemies, every alien (demon) that inhabits your being or is outside that controls your circumstances.

6. Humble ourselves and accept that God has been righteous in ordering our life and that He will bring it into the place He wants.

7. Remember He made covenants with Abraham, Isaac, and Jacob. Through Jesus Christ, His Son, we have a covenant. It is through Jesus Christ that we can be cleansed forever.

God is just and righteous. I believe as we confess our sins, iniquities and transgressions that God will forgive us, because we have access through our High Priest through the atoning blood. We need to declare what God has done and will do in our lives. We need to begin to tell others what He has done for us.

Is 43:25-28

"I, even I, am he that blotteth out thy transgressions for mine own sake, and will not remember thy sins. Put me in remembrance: let us plead together: declare thou, that thou mayest be justified. Thy first father hath sinned, and thy teachers have transgressed against me. Therefore I have profaned the princes of the sanctuary, and have given Jacob to the curse, and Israel to reproaches."

Let us declare to God that our forefathers have sinned. Let us apply the blood of Jesus Christ over our forefather's sins and ours. As we pray out loud and confess that our ancestors and we have sinned and our problems stem from iniquities, which became a curse. Then, acknowledging that Jesus Christ's shed blood is the only escape from our present situation. Thank Jesus for the cross and the blood and water that came from His side. Through the blood we are cleansed and made clean. Let us break free now in the name of Jesus.

PRAYER

Father, in the name of Jesus Christ, I come to you sincerely with the desire to be free from all curses, sins, iniquities, transgressions and their results. Lord Jesus, I thank you that I am a child of yours, that You saved me and You are cleansing me from my sin through the cross. I confess with my mouth that I belong to You, that the devil has no power over me because I am cleansed and covered by Your precious blood.

I recognize and now confess all of my sins and iniquities and transgressions known and unknown to me. *(Begin to repent of the things that you know that you have done—all perverseness, idolatry, divination, witchcraft, not obeying the commandments of the Lord, all the things our forefathers have done)* I repent now, Lord Jesus. I ask You to forgive me of those sins, iniquities and transgressions. I ask the Holy Spirit to further bring any of them to my remembrance that I have not confessed. Anything that I have missed, bring them to my remembrance.

I now, Lord Jesus, humbly confess the sins, iniquities and transgressions of all my forefathers. In the Name and by the power of the blood, I confess them, break them, renounce them. I command every demonic spirit, every spirit that would alienate and keep me from the blessings and promises of God to be loosed from me now. In the Name of Jesus they will not be passed down to my generations below me. They will stop here. Thank you Jesus!

In the Name of Jesus, I break the power and the hold of every curse that came down to me through sins, iniquities and transgressions of my forefathers, now!

Thank You Jesus as I renounce, break and loose myself and family from all demonic subjection, as a result of iniquities that have cursed me down to this generation.

Thank you Jesus for liberating me so these iniquities will not dominate, nor control me any longer, contrary to the Way and Will of God.

I break and declare every legal hold and ground of the enemy broken and destroyed. Satan no longer has a legal right to harass me, or my family line, through sins, iniquities or transgression because of the Blood of Jesus Christ.

I declare that I am free.

In the Name of Jesus Christ, I command all demonic spirits that have come in through curses of iniquities, sins, or transgressions leave me now. I say to you, GO, in Jesus Name, by the power of His Blood.

In the Name of Jesus Christ, I confess that my body, soul and spirit are the dwelling place of the Holy Ghost. I have been redeemed now and cleansed, sanctified, and justified by the Blood of Jesus Christ.

Jesus, I thank You for cleansing and setting me free. Amen!

Now any demonic spirit that came in through these sins, transgressions, and iniquities let them go by taking a deep breath and blowing them out, or if you feel like coughing, yawning, ears popping, or belching let it happen. You may not even sense anything but have a feeling of freedom, as if a load has been lifted. This is Jesus liberating you from many years of bondage.

Amen!

Chapter Three

So That's Why I'm Sick?

From the fall of Adam, sin came in and sickness came afterwards, then disease and poverty. All of these came into the world because of the fall. There are many things that entered the human race because of the fall. Things we have not dealt with in our particular lives. Because of the sins of our forefathers, these sins, iniquities and transgressions cause us to receive sicknesses in our bodies. There seems to be more sickness in the church today than is in the world. Go to the hospitals and you will see many Christians with sicknesses this should not be.

The Lord wants to heal us from sickness and disease. He wants us to walk with our life submitted to Him in every area. So He can heal us from all of our diseases.

The Word of God shows us many diseases. And we allow them in our lives. Some we see readily and others are alluded to. Sin opens up doors for diseases and sickness.

Devils have legal right to enter and inflict us with various ailments because of our sins.

Behind every physical ailment there is spiritual substance. Something spiritual caused the natural to happen. Every time we get attacked in our bodies, there is a spiritual force that we have allowed to attack us in that particular area of our body.

Let us look in Psalm 6

Ps 6:6-7

"I am weary with my groaning; all the night make I my bed to swim; I water my couch with my tears. Mine eye is consumed because of grief; it waxeth old because of all mine enemies."

Let's look at GRIEF.

He is talking about grief. What does grief affect? It affects your heart. There is a time for grief, like when someone dies, but there is a time to stop. If you go on past that particular time of grieving, it will affect your heart. But it not only affects your heart it says, "…mine eye is consumed…" so it also affects your eyesight. It not only can affect your natural eyesight but also your spiritual eyesight. It will also affect your bones.

Many people grieve over a divorce or loosing a loved one but instead of moving on they keep grieving and it affects them.

Grief is a spirit. It is a demonic hold and if we go beyond the time God allows for grief then this spirit will take hold. In Ecclesiastes it says there is a time for all things under the sun. We must see how long we have been grieving and then stop it. If we cannot stop then there is a demonic force behind it and that will affect our hearts, eyes and bones.

Here is another thing on grief.

Ps 31:9-10:

"Have mercy upon me, O LORD, for I am in trouble: mine eye is consumed with grief, yea, my soul and my belly."

Here, David is bringing up two other areas that are affected by grief—the soul man where the spirit of grief comes in when the door is open. Remember we are a tri-partite body—spirit, soul and body. Once we are saved our spirit man becomes alive again to the voice of God. We begin to experience the voice of God and have communion with Him. But we still have our soul man to contend with and our flesh. There are many people who have trouble with their flesh, their flesh has a hold of them. Our soul is our emotions, mind, will, and desires. So our emotions are having trouble. In the belly there are nerves, gastric problems. There can be disorders there as well.

"For my life is spent with grief, and my years with sighing: my strength faileth because of mine iniquity, and my bones are consumed."

People who sigh a lot show grief. It also shows that the bones can be consumed with grief. Iniquity has to be dealt with (Chapter 2). We have to deal with the sin we knowingly committed. What is that sin? Grieving beyond the time we should have grieved. Grief attacks the whole man—spirit, soul and body.

Look in Job.

Job 17:7:

"Mine eye also is dim by reason of <u>sorrow</u>, and all my members are as a shadow."

"Mine Eye," I believe it is not only the natural eye but also the spiritual eye. I believe it affects your spiritual seeing. The word sorrow is grief. So by reason of his grief, all his members are a shadow.

Again, if you have grief that has gone beyond what it should then a spirit of grief needs to be cast out.

Deuteronomy 28 talks about the blessings and curses. If we obey the voice of the Lord then we have the blessings but if we do not obey then we have the curses. Some people would like to think the Old has been done away with but the Word of God is the same yesterday, today and forever. His Word will never change.

As Paul said to Timothy in 2 Timothy 3:16,17:

"All scripture is given by inspiration of God, and is profitable for doctrine, for reproof, for correction, for instruction in righteousness: That the man of God may be perfect, throughly furnished unto all good works."

So in chapter 28 of Deuteronomy we see the blessings and curses. In verse 65, *"And among these nations shalt thou find no ease, neither shall the sole of thy foot have rest: but the LORD shall give thee there a trembling heart, and failing of eyes, and sorrow of mind."*

What does the eye show us? **Grief.**

Lam 5:16-17:

"The crown is fallen from our head: woe unto us, that we have sinned! For this our heart is faint; for these things our eyes are dim."

Here again is grief. So in dealing with grief, our eyes become dim both physically and spiritually.

In **Grief,** we deal with:

Depression, sorrow, sadness, melancholy, oppression, trembling heart, faint hearted, heartache, misery, agony, anguish, distress, despair, heaviness, gloominess, and sighing.

These are things that go with grief, they run together.

God wants us healthy in our bodies. We should deal with these spirits Father God has shown us.

Back in chapter 2 of Lamentations, verse 11, we find Jeremiah saying, *"Mine eyes do fail with tears, my bowels are troubled, my liver is poured upon the earth, for the destruction of the daughter of my people; because the children and the sucklings swoon in the streets of the city."*

He talks about the eyes. Jeremiah is grieving. It is a sad state to see the people of God in sickness. We should desire to see people free from all sicknesses.

Prov 14:30:

"A sound heart is the life of the flesh: but envy the rottenness of the bones."

Let's look at ENVY.

When you think of rottenness, what do you think of? I think of decay. Our bones would begin to decay and have problems. If we have a sound heart and our heart is right before the Lord, then we will not have this problem. Envy causes our bones to decay or waste away.

Jealousy, envy, and covetousness run together. They can cause our bones to rot and waste away.

Prov 12:4

"A virtuous woman is a crown to her husband: but she that maketh ashamed is as rottenness in his bones."

If there is trouble in a marriage, it will affect the bones of the couple.

What is in the bone? Bone marrow. There are various **cancers** in the bone. Our teeth are bone so tooth decay is affected. **Arthritis** can affect the bones. There are many things that are in the bones.

What things bring on arthritis? **Unforgiveness, resentment, bitterness, and covetousness bring on arthritis.**

We need to understand what brings different sicknesses on and begin to deal with each.

We read this earlier, but go back to Psalm 31.

Ps 31:10:

"For my life is spent with grief, and my years with sighing: my strength faileth because of mine iniquity, and my bones are consumed."

Our bones begin to dry up and shrink when we get older. There is also osteoporosis we get when we are older. I believe God wants to give us fat, healthy bones.

Prov 15:30:

"The light of the eyes rejoiceth the heart: and a good report maketh the bones fat."

We need to have good reports. To say good things about others and fatten their bones up.

Prov 16:24:

"Pleasant words are as an honeycomb, sweet to the soul, and health to the bones."

When someone has an evil report against you, do you come against them? We shouldn't! The scripture says, **"A soft answer turns away wrath."** Pleasant words are sweetness to the soul and will bring healthy bones.

Prov 18:20-21

"A man's belly shall be satisfied with the fruit of his mouth; and with the increase of his lips shall he be filled. Death and life are in the power of the tongue: and they that love it shall eat the fruit thereof."

We need to watch the very words that come from our mouths. We need to be aware of whether we are bringing life or death to the person or situation. Even to those who do not know the Lord, we need to speak life to them.

Ps 109:17-18:

"As he loved cursing, so let it come unto him: as he delighted not in blessing, so let it be far from him. As he clothed himself with cursing like as with his garment, so let it come into his bowels like water, and like oil into his bones."

As a man begins to love cursing then cursing will come unto his bones and will be a garment to him. It comes upon us, right into the emotional areas (bowels) and it is like oil in the bones. Cursing can cause bowel trouble. Those of us, who in days past, have cursed, need to repent and break the curse from us so we do not have bowel problems.

What bowel problems are there? There is **diarrhea, upset stomach, gas, colitis, hernia, monthly cycle problems, cancer of the colon, and spastic colon.** These come because of cursing others.

In Lamentations again.

Lam 1:20:

"Behold, O LORD; for I am in distress: my bowels are troubled; mine heart is turned within me; for I have grievously rebelled: abroad the sword bereaveth, at home there is as death."

Let's look at REBELLION.

Here we find rebellion causes problems. If we have rebelled against the Word of the Lord then our bowels will be troubled.

Let us inquire about a **spirit of jealousy**. Look in Numbers 5. This is what God told Moses to tell the priests, of that day, on how to judge jealousy.

Num 5:19-25:

"And the priest shall charge her by an oath, and say unto the woman, If no man have lain with thee, and if thou hast not gone aside to uncleanness with another instead of thy husband, be thou free from this bitter water that causeth the curse: But if thou hast gone aside to another instead of thy husband, and if thou be defiled, and some man have lain with thee beside thine husband: Then the priest shall charge the woman with an oath of cursing, and the priest shall say unto the woman, The LORD make thee a curse and an oath among thy people, when the LORD doth make thy thigh to rot, and thy belly to swell; And this water that causeth the curse shall go into thy bowels, to make thy belly to swell, and thy thigh to rot: And the woman shall say, Amen, amen. And the priest shall write these curses in a book, and he shall blot them out with the bitter water:
And he shall cause the woman to drink the bitter water that causeth the curse: and the water that causeth the curse shall enter into her, and become bitter."

Let's look at JEALOUSY.

If there was a man who thought his wife was cheating on him and she denied it and he was jealous then he would go to the priest. There was special water they had to drink. The woman had to drink it. She took the oath and swore that she did not lay with any other man. If she were lying then her lower extremities and her belly would swell up. If her belly did not swell up then she was telling truth and she was not defiled and she was free to conceive the seed from her husband.

Any person that commits an act of adultery, a curse enters into them. The spirit of jealousy will enter in as well.

The scripture uses a woman as one who is committing adultery but it also goes for a man.

The stomach is that which speaks of the seed of the **appetite** and **digestive** problems.

Num 5:14

"And the spirit of jealousy come upon him, and he be jealous of his wife, and she be defiled: or if the spirit of jealousy come upon him, and he be jealous of his wife, and she be not defiled."

This spirit will cause problems. Adultery always causes problems.

We read about the works of the flesh in Galatians 5: 19: *"Now the works of the flesh are manifest, which are these; Adultery, fornication, uncleanness, lasciviousness."*

These four are sexual sins and will cause the spirit of jealousy to come and result in problems. It causes problems for those who are not committed or not true to their spouse. It will cause problems in their bellies, in their thighs and in their sexual reproductive systems.

Let us look at the spirit of bitterness.

Isa 38:1-5

"In those days was Hezekiah sick unto death. And Isaiah the prophet the son of Amoz came unto him, and said unto him, Thus saith the LORD, Set thine house in order: for thou shalt die, and not live."

How would you like it if a prophet came and told you because of your sin you are going to die?

"Then Hezekiah turned his face toward the wall, and prayed unto the LORD."

He knew it was a true word from God so he repented.

"And said, Remember now, O LORD, I beseech thee, how I have walked before thee in truth and with a perfect heart, and have done that which is good in thy sight. And Hezekiah wept sore. Then came the word of the LORD to Isaiah, saying, Go, and say to Hezekiah, Thus saith the LORD, the God of David thy father, I have heard thy prayer, I have seen thy tears: behold, I will add unto thy days fifteen years."

Hezekiah had a spirit of bitterness. He was sick but the Lord turned it around because he repented. Hezekiah was given 15 more years. In that time span, Hezekiah had a son born called Menes. Menes was one of the most wicked kings in Israel.

Isa 38:17:

"Behold, for peace I had great bitterness: but thou hast in love to my soul delivered it from the pit of corruption: for thou hast cast all my sins behind thy back."

Isa 38:15 :

"What shall I say? He hath both spoken unto me, and himself hath done it: I shall go softly all my years in the bitterness of my soul."

Hezekiah was bitter; even though he was healed there was still bitterness. It was in his soul.

Why does God deliver you? Because He loves you and because of His mercy. He loved Hezekiah but because of the bitterness in his soul, his life would be taken.

Isa 38:21

"For Isaiah had said, Let them take a lump of figs, and lay it for a plaister upon the boil, and he shall recover."

So, what did Hezekiah have with his bitterness? **Boils**! Bitterness can bring on **skin disorders** and **diseases**. Bitterness can be resentment. We can be **sullen** and **spiteful**. We can be **crabby, sour, scornful, mean, ugly, angry, and rancorous**. All these things can affect our bodies. There are **boils, lumps, bumps, acne, and skin cancers** that can come up because of bitterness and envy.

Let's look at VANITY.

Have you ever had a problem sleeping? Sometimes it can be because of what we ate or when we ate. Most of the time though, when we have problems sleeping it can be because of **witchcraft**. We have dealt with people who have problems sleeping and it was because of witchcraft.

Job 7:3-5

"So am I made to possess months of vanity, and wearisome nights are appointed to me. When I lie down, I say, When shall I arise, and the night be gone? And I am full of tossings to and fro unto the dawning of the day. My flesh is clothed with worms and clods of dust; my skin is broken, and become loathsome."

Months of vanities, he says. Vanity can produce insomnia and the inability to sleep. We need to be profitable in what God wants us to do.

Restlessness brings about **hopelessness, despair, anxiety, and futility**. If you are tossing to and fro then you are going to be restless during the day.

I believe there are prayers that are prayed by witches and warlocks and those in satanic covens that can keep us awake also.

Let's look at the spirits of haughtiness and pride.

These can cause skin problems. In Isaiah 3, we see the Prophet beginning to talk to the daughters of Zion.

Isa 3:16, 17, 24

"Moreover the LORD saith, Because the daughters of Zion are haughty, and walk with stretched forth necks and wanton eyes, walking and mincing as they go, and making a tinkling with their feet: Therefore the LORD will smite with a scab the crown of the head of the daughters of Zion, and the LORD will discover their secret parts. And it shall come to pass, that instead of sweet smell there shall be stink; and instead of a girdle a rent; and instead of well set hair baldness; and instead of a stomacher a girding of sackcloth; and burning instead of beauty."

We see the **spirits of haughtiness, pride, boasting and arrogance.** Some of this runs with the spirit of Jezebel. The word *Zion* can be translated—the church. The daughters of the church are haughty and high-minded and the Lord is going to smite them with a scab on the crown of their heads. Here it speaks of **eczema, cirrhosis, scalp problems, loosing hair, baldness, female cancers, stench, bad odors, and venereal disease.**

God said He would see their secret parts and that brings **AIDS, harlotry, fornication, seduction, and infections in the sexual organs.** These are all curses because of haughtiness and pride. Remember in Proverbs16:18; it says that **"Pride goeth before destruction and an haughty spirit before a fall."** We need to watch our hearts and ask the Lord if there is haughtiness in us. Haughtiness means, Am I lifting my self up instead of Christ Jesus? Is there any pride in our heart? If so Lord reveal it to us.

Have you noticed that some women's hair is very thin, even some baldness. I am talking about women in their 30s to 50s. This prompted me think that there is a spirit of haughtiness there.

Isa 2:11

"The lofty looks of man shall be humbled, and the haughtiness of men shall be bowed down, and the LORD alone shall be exalted in that day."

"Bowed down" would be like osteoporosis. There are many things that can come in because of haughtiness in our life.

Ps 73:21

"Thus my heart was grieved, and I was pricked in my reins." (Reins—inner body, especially kidneys)

Jer 17:10-11

"I the LORD search the heart, I try the reins, even to give every man according to his ways, and according to the fruit of his doings. As the

partridge sitteth on eggs, and hatcheth them not; so he that getteth riches, and not by right, shall leave them in the midst of his days, and at his end shall be a fool."

Rev 2:23

"And I will kill her children with death; and all the churches shall know that I am he which searcheth the reins and hearts: and I will give unto every one of you according to your works."

The "reins" also means our minds, our inward parts. With a horse, the reins determine how fast and what direction the horse is going. The horse is trained to do exactly what the master says. The Lord wants to deliver and heal our minds and cause us to go His direction.

What do our kidneys do? They eliminate poisons. There are kidney stones and other diseases involving the kidney. If our kidneys are functioning right then the poisons are going out of our system. If the kidneys are not functioning right then the poisons are staying in our system and causes many other problems.

We can have problems in our emotions, in the gall bladder, and many other areas because of a build up of poison in our system. Gallstones and kidney stones can also be a sign of bitterness (Hebrews 12:15). If the gall bladder malfunctions then it can cause problems in our digestive system.

Sickness can come on us gradually. We can go to bed feeling well and wake up sick. Have you ever noticed how sickness comes on the body at nighttime? It comes upon you at your weakest time. Is that not like Satan? He always hits us at our weakest time.

Remember the story of Miriam when she stood up against Moses (Numbers 12)? What happened? She immediately came down with leprosy. Leprosy came because she reviled the ministry of Moses. She was upset because Moses was not doing things her way. She stood up against God's authority. Had it not been for Moses, her brother, interceding for her she would have gone to her grave with leprosy. Those who speak out against God's anointed are inflicted with disease! Beware what you say about the anointed vessels of God.

Overworking causes sickness?

Your immune system gets weak and can not fight off the germs.

Phil 2:25-30

"Yet I supposed it necessary to send to you Epaphroditus, my brother, and companion in labour, and fellow soldier, but your messenger, and he that ministered to my wants. For he longed after you all, and was

80

full of heaviness, because that ye had heard that he had been sick. For indeed he was sick nigh unto death: but God had mercy on him; and not on him only, but on me also, lest I should have sorrow upon sorrow. I sent him therefore the more carefully, that, when ye see him again, ye may rejoice, and that I may be the less sorrowful. Receive him therefore in the Lord with all gladness; and hold such in reputation: Because for the work of Christ he was nigh unto death, not regarding his life, to supply your lack of service toward me."

Here is a man that was desirous on doing the work of the Lord, to see his brothers and sisters come into knowledge and truth, that he overworked himself and almost died.

Most people do not understand the desire of women and men of God who minister. There is such a desire in their hearts to help people that they weary themselves. They do not get the proper rest or food. They minister late to the early hours. They become weary. We must be careful and get the proper rest.

Let us look at RAGE.

Look in 2 Chronicles 16. Asa was reigning at this time.

81

2 Chr 16:7-12:

"And at that time Hanani the seer came to Asa king of Judah, and said unto him, Because thou hast relied on the king of Syria, and not relied on the LORD thy God, therefore is the host of the king of Syria escaped out of thine hand. Were not the Ethiopians and the Lubims a huge host, with very many chariots and horsemen? yet, because thou didst rely on the LORD, he delivered them into thine hand. For the eyes of the LORD run to and fro throughout the whole earth, to shew himself strong in the behalf of them whose heart is perfect toward him. Herein thou hast done foolishly: therefore from henceforth thou shalt have wars. Then Asa was wroth with the seer, and put him in a prison house; for he was in a rage with him because of this thing. And Asa oppressed some of the people the same time. And, behold, the acts of Asa, first and last, lo, they are written in the book of the kings of Judah and Israel. And Asa in the thirty and ninth year of his reign was diseased in his feet, until his disease was exceeding great: yet in his disease he sought not to the LORD, but to the physicians."

We find several things here with Asa. First, he came against the seer or the prophet of God. He did not like the truth coming from the prophet of God. He said, "You stopped trusting the Lord and started trusting in yourself. Because of these things you are going to have wars continually." Asa did not like to hear this. So he had the prophet of God put into a house prison. This way he did not have to hear him but the Word of the Lord had already been spoken. Verse 9 says *"the eye of the Lord looks to and fro for a heart that is perfect."* Lord, let our heart be perfect towards you. Let our mind be staid upon you. Let us do the things you desire and not our desires.

Because Asa did not trust in the Lord, he was cursed. We find in verse 12 that he did not go to God at all. He did not seek the Lord concerning this matter. He was diseased in his feet. His walk life was terrible. He walked away from his Lord. Asa was enraged because of this. Rage has something to do with our feet. If people have trouble with their feet, there is rage in them. Those who have rage in their heart need help.

Doctors are a gift from God but, we need to go to the Lord first. Verse 12 is our example. *"He sought not the Lord but to the physicians."* Those in the medical profession need to direct people to the Lord first, remembering they are but a tool of God's. A doctor who says he heals is wrong, he can only mend God heals.

What brings in rage?

Proverbs 20: 1: *"Wine is a mocker, strong drink is raging: and whosoever is deceived thereby is not wise."*

A mocking spirit comes in through winebibbers. They that use such begin to mock others, then mock the things of God.

There is lack of wisdom from using alcohol. Those who call upon the name of the Lord should abstain.

Strong drink, beer, whisky, gin, vodka, etc.,brings in rage. Look at a person who is mild-mannered then they consume some alcohol and become enraged, destructive, abusive, loud mouthed, looking for trouble and full of anger. As has been stated rage will cause problems in your feet, not only natural but spiritual, causing you to walk away from Father God.

Let us look at leprosy.

II Kings 5:21-27:

"So Gehazi followed after Naaman [Naaman was cured with his skin disease, his leprosy. Elisha did not want any payment for healing Naaman but Gehazi decided he did.] *And when Naaman saw him running after him, he lighted down from the chariot to meet him, and said, Is all well? And he said, All is well. My master hath sent me,* [he lied] *saying, Behold, even now there be come to me from mount Ephraim two young men of the sons of the prophets: give them, I pray thee, a talent of silver, and two changes of garments.*

And Naaman said, Be content, take two talents. And he urged him, and bound two talents of silver in two bags, with two changes of garments, and laid them upon two of his servants; and they bare them before him. And when he came to the tower, he took them from their hand, and bestowed them in the house: and he let the men go, and they departed. But he went in, and stood before his master. And Elisha said unto him, Whence comest thou, Gehazi? And he said, Thy servant went no whither. And he said unto him, Went not mine heart with thee, when the man turned again from his chariot to meet thee? Is it a time to receive money, and to receive garments, and olive yards, and vineyards, and sheep, and oxen, and menservants, and maidservants? The leprosy therefore of Naaman shall cleave unto thee, and unto thy seed forever. And he went out from his presence a leper as white as snow."

Here is a curse that came from the prophet to Gehazi to his seed forever. Gehazi was coveting and then lied. Because of these things he was cursed. We see in Zechariah 5:3-4, the curse that goes over the face of the earth to those who lie.

We know curses can be broken through the name of Jesus, only!

Let us look at Uzziah.

2 Chr 26:16-21

"But when he was strong, his heart was lifted up to his destruction: for he transgressed against the LORD his God, and went into the temple of the LORD to burn incense upon the altar of incense. [Who was to go into the temple? The priest only.] *And Azariah the priest went in after him, and with him fourscore priests of the LORD, that were valiant men: And they withstood Uzziah the king, and said unto him, It appertaineth not unto thee, Uzziah, to burn incense unto the LORD, but to the priests the sons of Aaron, that are consecrated to burn incense: go out of the sanctuary; for thou hast trespassed; neither shall it be for thine honour from the LORD God. Then Uzziah was wroth, and had a censer in his hand to burn incense: and while he was wroth with the priests, the leprosy even rose up in his forehead before the priests in the house of the LORD, from beside the incense altar. And Azariah the chief priest, and all the priests, looked upon him, and, behold, he was leprous in his forehead, and they thrust him out from thence; yea, himself hasted also to go out, because the LORD had smitten him. And Uzziah the king was a leper unto the day of his death, and dwelt in a several house, being a leper; for he was cut off from the house of the LORD: and Jotham his son was over the king's house, judging the people of the land."*

Uzziah pushed himself into the ministry. He decided he was going to be the priest of the Lord. There are many who thrust themselves into ministry but are not called.

Presumptuous, self-willed with no anointing for service to the Lord.

- Uzziah was rebellious, responsible and religious.
- He was rebellious because he pushed himself into a ministry with no calling.
- He was responsible because he presumed to walk in an office not of his calling.
- He was religious because he touched the altar of incense not being an anointed vessel for this calling.
- His presumption caused his leprosy and death. The curse followed his lineage to the third and fourth generation.

There are those God has called into ministry and there are those who think they should be in ministry, speaking of the five fold ministry (Ephesians 4:11). They have a religious spirit and think they are called and chosen of God. Those the Lord has called and chosen have the anointing and because of the anointing the yoke in people's lives can be broken.

Another way sickness comes is by not judging ourselves before we partake of communion. We should examine ourselves before we partake.

1 Cor 11:28-32

"But let a man examine himself, and so let him eat of that bread, and drink of that cup.

For he that eateth and drinketh unworthily, eateth and drinketh damnation to himself, not discerning the Lord's body.

For this cause many are weak and sickly among you, and many sleep.

For if we would judge ourselves, we should not be judged.

But when we are judged, we are chastened of the Lord, that we should not be condemned with the world."

Sicknesses and diseases come in when we do not open ourselves up before the Lord and ask to be seen as He sees us.

Jesus wants us to take communion it is an important part of our Christian walk. But we need to examine ourselves before we take it. We need to acknowledge to the Lord our sins and say, "I know I have sinned. I know I have fallen short of the glory. Lord, I ask you to forgive me of my sins." We should do this as often as we do communion. If we do not sickness can come upon us. Even weakness or death could come. If we look at it spiritually there are many who are weak in their faith. They except wrong doctrine and through deception believe anything.

We need to judge ourselves daily. We know the Lord is our deliverer and our healer, He wants us free. Jesus paid the price, 100%, by His precious blood, and by His stripes we appropriate our healing.

Thank God for what Jesus did for us. He walked perfect in the sight of God. Can you say you have? But we are striving to walk in a more perfect way. Striving to watch what we say. Striving to keep ourself pure and clean from the world and not allow the world to enter in the church. Striving to do things according to God's ways and not according to man's.

We find in Isaiah 53:4-5, *"Surely he hath borne our griefs, and carried our sorrows: yet we did esteem him stricken, smitten of God, and afflicted. But he was wounded for our transgressions, he was bruised for our iniquities: the chastisement of our peace was upon him; and with his stripes we are healed."*

These are just a few examples, scripturally, of the many sickness' which are in the Body of Christ and bring curses on individuals and families. As we say "It's Easy With Jesus," if we will but obey and turn from our wicked ways and repent of those of our ancesters. The Lord Jesus has made a way of escape, we need to appropriate His way for the release of diseases in our lives. To repent means to turn around and run the other way. So Repent, Repent, Repent.

PRAYER

Lord Jesus, I come to you and acknowledge I have transgressed Your Word. Lord, I have not followed Your Word aggressively. I, in some way, have opened up my heart to cause spirits to enter bringing in disease and sickness. I repent for grieving beyond the time of grieving. I have opened up my eyes for destruction and opened up my bones for destruction. I ask you to forgive, deliver and set me free.

I ask if there is any bitterness or resentment in my heart, to forgive those who have hurt me as I forgive them, to deliver and set me free. Jesus, I ask for deliverance from my heart and mind of any resentment or bitterness that causes cancers, acne, sores or any other disease or sickness.

I ask You, Lord, if I have allowed haughtiness and pride into my life, to be delivered from these. I do not want to be boastful in my own eye, or be arrogant.

Lord, I ask that you deliver me from diseases in my scalp, hair, and sexual organs. I ask for your deliverance.

I break the curses that have come into my life in the Name of Jesus.

If I have in anyway allowed rage into my life, I ask for forgiveness. I ask you to forgive for opening this door.

I ask that you would heal my feet and would walk the path you desire me to walk and be not contrary to Your Word.

I ask you for deliverance from all rage, anger and bitterness.

If I have been in error or stood against the true prophets of God, I ask you to forgive in the Name of Jesus. Deliver me, Lord, so no leprosy will come upon me or my children, to the third and fourth generation.

I ask you would forgive our ancestors of their transgressions, iniquities, and any sins they have committed. I break the power of those curses that came in through, iniquities and transgressions. Set me free in Jesus' Name.

Lord, forgive me for sinning against you; for doing things my own way and not doing them according to Your ways, in Jesus' Name.

For Your hand is not slack, thank You for delivering me now of all spirits that have entered into my soulish nature, in Jesus' Name.

Amen!

Chapter Four

What's in My Bloodline!

In Paul's first writing to the Corinthians he was not able to speak unto them spiritual. Because of them staying yet babes in Christ.

I Corinthians 3: 1-2;

"And I, brethren, could not speak unto you as unto spiritual, but as unto carnal, even as babes in Christ. I have fed you with milk, and not with meat: for hitherto ye were not able to bear it, neither yet now are ye able."

Many Christians are weak in the faith. In an era which has more opportunity to become strong in the Word, we are the weakest. Many are content to stay were they are in their salvation experience. Never getting past their Born-Again experience. Most filling the pulpits never move past the milk stage of feeding the flock. We can almost know from week to week the order of ministry, no room for the Holy Spirit to move. Most messages feed our intellect and not our spirit.

Yet, there are a hungry few who desire to pursue a deeper walk with the Lord. It is to those hungering for the meat this book is being written. A steady diet of the same thing causes us to get complacent, lethargic, and down right sluggish in our spiritual walk. As in the natural, milk will only let us grow to a certain level. But add the meat and watch us grow! So, in the spiritual, we need the meat.

Hebrews 5:13-14 states;

"For every one that useth milk is unskilful in the word of righteousness: for he is a babe. But strong meat belongeth to them that are of full age, even them who by reason of use have their senses exercised to discern both good and evil."

Let us look at our bloodline to determine the causes of problems in our lives. As in the previous chapter, we must deal with our iniquities. Now that we have become aware of our ancestral iniquities, let's look at curses coming as a result.

In Deuteronomy 28: 1-2:

"And it shall come to pass, if thou shalt hearken diligently unto the voice of the Lord thy God, to observe and to do all his commandments which I command thee this day, that the Lord thy God will set thee on high above all nations of the earth. And all these blessings shall come on thee, and overtake thee, if thou shalt hearken unto the voice of the Lord thy God."

Blessings bring with it exaltation (being lifted up), health, reproductiveness in every area, prosperity, victory, and God's favor.

Blessings of God should be evident in every Christian's life.

The basic causes of all blessings are listening to God's voice and doing what He says.

The opposite of a blessing is a curse.

Deuteronomy 28: 15 lists the basic cause for curses: *"But it shall come to pass, if thou wilt not hearken unto the voice of the Lord thy God, to observe to do all his commandments and his statutes which I command thee this day, that all these curses shall come upon thee, and overtake thee ...."*

The root cause for curses in our lives is not hearing and not obeying God's voice.

Curses bring with it humiliation, failure to reproduce (barrenness in almost any area is the outworking of a curse), mental and physical sickness, family breakdown, poverty, defeat, oppression, failure, and God's disfavor.

Notice both blessings and curses "overtake us," we do not have to pursue them, just fulfill the conditions, either positive or negative. We can never go fast enough as that they will not overtake us!

Look at your life and verify what is working.

Almost 30 years ago I asked the Lord, "Why are we having so many problems in our lives." Not knowing the outlying problem was not something physical that could be seen but a spiritual force not detected with the human faculties.

In my years of ministry have found that blessings and curses are not limited to single individuals but are related to a family, a community, a nation, or sometimes a whole civilization.

In Proverbs 26: 2 it states;

"As the bird by wandering, as the swallow by flying, so the curse causeless shall not come."

Wherever a curse alights there is a cause behind it. It is important to discover the cause, which is why this chapter is so important to believers.

Derek Prince indicates in his book *From Curse to Blessing* a list of seven common indications to a curse in the lives of people.

1. Mental and/or emotional breakdown.

2. Repeated or chronic sicknesses, especially if they are hereditary or without clear medical diagnosis.

3. Repeated miscarriages or related female problems.

4.   The breakdown of marriage and family alienation; where a family falls apart.

5.   Continuing financial insufficiency, especially where the income appears to be sufficient.

6.   Being accident-prone.

7.   In a family, a history of suicides or unnatural deaths.

We had already been exposed to these phenomena via the Holy Spirit prior to picking up Derek's book. In fact we had a bible study in which we all looked up areas of either blessings or curses in scripture. From this study time we compiled a list of biblical curses, which are important enough not to deny. And have listed these on the next few pages.

BIBLICAL CURSES

Biblical Curses—Sins and Acts that Constitute a Curse:

(This is not an exhaustive list)

"...The curse causeless shall not come..."
Proverbs 26: 2

1. Those that curse or mistreat God's chosen people of any generation.
    Genesis 12: 3; 27: 29; Numbers 24: 9

2. Those who are willing deceivers **(especially those who deceive God's people)**.
    Genesis 27: 12; Joshua 9: 22-23; Jeremiah 48: 10; Malachi 1: 14

3. An adulterous woman **(harlot, prostitute)**.
    Numbers 5: 27

4. Disobedience to the Lord's Commandments **(His Word)**.
    Deuteronomy 11: 28; Jeremiah 11: 3; Daniel 9: 11

5. Idolatry **(worshiping or esteeming something or someone above the living God, including secret societies)**.

   Exodus 20: 3-5; Deuteronomy 5: 8; 29: 19-20; Jeremiah 44: 8

6. Those who keep or own cursed objects. Deuteronomy

   7: 25-26; Joshua 6: 18

7. Those that refuse to come to the Lord's help **(fight for the Lord)**.

   Judges 5: 23

8. House of the wicked **(if God's blessing is not there, the curse is)**.

   Proverbs 3: 33

9. He who does not give to the poor.

   Proverbs 28: 27

10. The earth, by reason of man's disobedience.

    Isaiah 24: 3-6

11. Jerusalem is a curse to all nations if Jews rebel against God.

    Jeremiah 26: 6

12. One who steals, or swears falsely by the Lord's name.

    Zechariah 5: 3-4

13. Ministers who fail to give the glory to God **(even their blessing will be cursed)**.

    Malachi 2: 2

14. Those who rob God of tithes and offerings **(not being honest with God concerning finances)**.

    Haggai 1: 6-9; Malachi 3:9; Acts 5: 1-11

15. Those who hearken unto their wives rather than God.

    Genesis 3: 17

16. Those who lightly esteem their parents **(dishonoring father and mother)**.

    Deuteronomy 27: 16

17. Those that make graven images **(one of the primary causes of curses--turning from God to the occult or a cult)**.

    Exodus 20: 4; Deuteronomy 5: 8; 27: 15

18. Those that willfully cheat people out of their property **(mistreating your neighbors)**.

    Deuteronomy 27: 17.

19. Those who take advantage of the blind **(wrong attitude toward the helpless)**.

    Deuteronomy 27: 18

20. Those that oppress strangers, widows, or the fatherless.

    Exodus 22: 22-24; Deuteronomy 27: 19

21. Him who lies with his father's wife **(incest)**.

    Deuteronomy 27: 20

22. Him who lies with any beast **(bestiality)**.

    Exodus 22: 19; Leviticus 20: 15-16; Deuteronomy 27: 21

23. Him who lies with his sister **(incest)**.

    Deuteronomy 27: 22

24. Those who smite their neighbors secretly **(murder)**.

    Deuteronomy 27: 24

25. Those who take money to slay the innocent **(murder for hire)**.

    Deuteronomy 27: 25

26. Adulterers **(extra-marital sex, rapists)**.

    Deuteronomy 22: 22-27; Job 24: 15-18

27. The proud **(an abomination to God -- He hates pride)**.

    Psalm 119: 21

28. Those that trust in man and not the Lord.

    Jeremiah 17: 5

29. Those who do the work of the Lord deceitfully **(slothfully)**.

    Jeremiah 48: 10

30. Him who keeps back his sword from blood **(refusal to fight [spiritual warfare] for the Lord)**.

    1 Kings 20: 35-42; Jeremiah 48:10

31. Those that reward evil for good.

    Proverbs 17: 13

32. Illegitimate children **(curse in effect for 10 generations—family curse)**.

    Deuteronomy 23: 2

33. Children born from incestuous unions.

    Genesis 19: 36-38

34. Murderers **(abortion, abortionists, advocates of abortion)**.

    Genesis 4: 11; Exodus 21: 12

35. To murder indirectly.

    Exodus 21: 14

36. Children who strike their parents.

    Exodus 21: 15

37. Kidnappers.

    Exodus 21: 16; Deuteronomy 24: 7

38. Those who curse **(swear with profanity)** their parents.

    Exodus 21: 17

39. Those that cause the unborn to die **(also abortion)**.

    Exodus 21: 22-23

40. Those that do not prevent death **(caused by an animal)**.

    Exodus 21: 29

41. Those who sacrifice to false gods.

    Exodus 22: 20

42. Those involved in witchcraft.

    Exodus 22: 18

43. Those who attempt to turn anyone away from the Lord.

    Deuteronomy 13: 6-9

44. Those that follow horoscopes and astrology.
    Deuteronomy 17: 2-5

45. Those that rebel against pastors.
    Deuteronomy 17: 12

46. False prophets.
    Deuteronomy 18: 19-22; 2 Peter 2: 12-14

47. Parents who do not discipline their children but honor them above God.
    1 Samuel 2: 17, 27-36

48. Women who do not keep their virginity until they are married.
    Deuteronomy 22: 13-21

49. Those who curse their rulers.
    Exodus 22: 28; 1 Kings 2: 8-9

50. Those who teach rebellion against the Lord.
    Jeremiah 28: 16-17

51. Those who refuse to warn people about sin.
    Ezekiel 3: 18-21

52. Those that defile the Sabbath.
    Exodus 31: 14; Numbers 15: 32-36

53. Those who sacrifice human beings.
    Leviticus 20: 2

54. Participants in séances and fortune telling.
    Leviticus 20: 6

55. Homosexual and lesbian relationships.
    Leviticus 20: 13; Romans 1: 26-32

56. Sexual intercourse during menstruation.
    Leviticus 20: 18

57. Necromancers **(praying to the dead)** and fortunetellers.
    Leviticus 20: 27; Deuteronomy 18: 10-12

58. Those who blaspheme the Lord's name.
    Leviticus 24: 15-16

59. Those that are carnally minded.

    Romans 8: 6

60. Sodomites.

    Genesis 19: 13, 24-25

61. Rebellious children.

    Deuteronomy 21: 18-21; Ephesians 6: 1-6

62. Pain in childbirth.

    Genesis 3: 16

63. Refusal to do or act upon the Word of God.

    Deuteronomy 27: 26

64. Family disorder.

    Malachi 4: 6

65. Failure and poverty.

    Haggai 1: 5-6

66. Sin worthy of death.

    Deuteronomy 21: 22-23

67. Those who devise iniquity.
    Micah 2: 1-3

68. "Touching" God's anointed.
    1 Chronicles 16: 22; Psalm 105: 15

69. Perversion of the Gospel of Christ.
    Galatians 1: 8-9

70. Those who love cursing, cursing comes upon them.
    Psalm 109: 17-20

71. Those that go down to Egypt **(world system)** for help and look not to the Lord.
    Isaiah 31: 1-3

72. Those that choose that which God does not delight in.
    Isaiah 65: 11-15

73. Stubbornness and rebellion.
    1 Samuel 15: 22-23

74. Those who offend children **(or anyone)** who

108

believe in Jesus Christ.

Matthew 18: 4-7

75. Those that add to or take away from the Word.

Deuteronomy 4: 2; Revelation 22: 18-19

76. Failure to hearken unto the voice of the Lord God, to observe to do all His commandments and His statutes.

Deuteronomy 28:16-68

"All these curses shall come upon thee, and overtake thee."

Notice that idolatry is one of the areas that bring in a curse. Worshipping false gods or occult practices will result in the same. Servants of God the Father should not seek out servants of false gods for help. This will only bring about a 3-4 generation curse.

Do you as a believer want to harm your children, grandchildren, or great-grandchildren?

Many may ask, "What will the result be from this curse." Much of the time we find diseases, bad acne, female problems to name a few.

Some people have a curse over their life because of a wrong attitude or relation-ship to their parents. The first commandment with blessing recorded in Ephesians 6:1-3: *"Children, obey your parents in the Lord: for this is right. Honour thy father and mother* [which is the first commandment with promise]; *That it may be well with thee, and thou mayest live long on the earth."*

If you fail to honor your parents, you incur a curse upon yourself. If that is your condition, you need to repent, change, adjust your attitude and if possible your relationship with your parents. A person with a wrong attitude toward their parents never comes under the full blessing of God.

Illicit or unnatural sex such as adultery, fornication, incest, homosexuality and bestiality will bring a curse into the bloodline. These are in more bloodlines than we would like to think. Am sure there is someone you may know who has been either a victim or perpetrator of such acts. The media has opened up the door for these to be propagated in our society. Just channel surf the TV to see if this is not the TRUTH. The Scripture informs us to help those who are in such a condition under the yoke of the devil.

As we see in 2 Tim 2:25-26, *"In meekness instructing those that oppose themselves; if God per-adventure will give them repentance to the acknowledging of the truth; And that they may recover themselves out of the snare of the devil, who are taken captive by him at his will."*

Those who are unjust to the weak or the helpless will fall under a curse. The most outstanding example is abortion—deliberate killing of unborn children. The people Father God had Israel remove from the promise land were those who did such atrocities. If you are guilty of this there is a curse over your life. Many have been apart of, given permission to, or preformed such. You must meet God's conditions for redemption from the curse; turn to God for mercy and escape from the curse.

The following is a prayer for those who have accepted Jesus Christ into their lives and desire to be free from the curse. Then deliverance comes to those who call upon the name of Jesus Christ for freedom.

Prayer and Confession
for the Breaking of Curses

The way of escaping CURSES and their results is through
RECOGNITION, REPENTANCE,
RENUNCIATION, and RESISTANCE.

Recognize that you have a problem and the only way out is
through Jesus Christ.

Repent of your sins and those of your ancestors and ask
God through His Son Jesus to forgive you and your
ancestors of all sins.

Renounce all past practices with your sin and those who
lead you into sin.

Resist the enemy and draw near to God, remember Satan
wants you back at any cost.

PRAYER FOR BREAKING OF CURSES

(Read out loud to give Satan and his demons notice that this is the end.)

Father, in the name of Jesus Christ, I come to you sincerely with a desire to be free from ALL curses, iniquities, transgressions and their results in My life.

Lord Jesus, thank you for saving me and cleansing away my sin at the Cross. I confess with my mouth that I belong to you. The devil has no power over me because I am cleansed and covered by your Precious Blood.

I recognize and now confess all my sins, iniquities, and transgressions known and unknown. I repent of them now in the Name of Jesus. I ask you Lord to forgive me of those sins, iniquities, and transgressions I remember and for the Holy Spirit to further bring to remembrance any I may have missed, now or in the near future, Thank you Lord Jesus.

I now confess the sins, iniquities, and transgressions of all my forefathers. In the Name and by the Blood of Jesus Christ, I break and renounce the power of every Demonic Curse that has passed down to me through the sins, iniquities, transgressions, and actions of others.

113

In the Name of Jesus Christ, I break the power and the hold of every curse which came to me through SIN, INIQUITY, and TRANSGRESSIONS; mine and those of my forefathers.

In the Name of Jesus Christ, I break the power and the hold of every curse that came to me through WORDS spoken, mine or those of others.

In the Name of Jesus Christ, I break the power and the hold of every curse that came to me through DISOBEDIENCE—my forefathers or mine.

In the Name of Jesus Christ, I now renounce, break, and loose myself and my family from ALL DEMONIC SUBJECTION to my father, mother, grandparents, or any other human being, living or dead, that have ever in the past or are now dominating or controlling me or my family in ANY WAY contrary to the Word and the will of God.

In the Name of Jesus Christ, I now renounce, break, and loose myself and my family from all psychic heredity, demonic strongholds, psychic powers, bondages; bonds of inherited physical or mental illness, or curses upon me and my family line as a result of sins, iniquities, transgressions, occult or psychic involvement of any member of my family line, living or dead.

In the Name of Jesus Christ, I declare every legal hold, and every legal ground of the enemy broken and destroyed. Satan NO LONGER has a legal right to harass my family line through curses. Through the Blood of Jesus Christ—I am free. Thank you Jesus, for setting me free.

In the Name of Jesus Christ, I command all demonic spirits that entered me through curses to begin to leave me now!! Go in the Name of Jesus Christ, by the power of His Blood, and by the power of the Holy Spirit.

I confess that my body, soul and spirit are the dwelling place of the Spirit of God. I am redeemed, cleansed, sanctified, and justified, by the Blood of Jesus Christ. Therefore neither Satan nor his demons have any place in power or me over me, because of the Blood of Jesus.

THANK YOU, JESUS, FOR SETTING ME FREE!

AMEN!